Healing Is A Gradient

Healing Is A
Gradient

A collection of poems, insights, mindset shifts, and the process of healing

by
Charlese Annette Phillips

First Edition, 2026
ISBN: 979-8-218-92988-6

Contact Charlese at www.charleseannette.com
Cover Art by Charlese Annette Phillips

This book is dedicated to those who have struggled to heal, struggled to love, struggled to feel, struggled to live, but choose to keep going.

If you're ever in need of help.
Call the suicide hotline at: 988

Contents

Introduction

This was not an easy book to write. And for many reasons as you will soon find out. The depths of myself I had to reach to get to a point of sharing these was soul-opening and foundation-breaking. I had to crumble, fully, to rebuild myself into a person who was even brave enough to share some of this story of mine. This book is a collection of poems I have written over the years. To be honest, I don't remember when I started writing them. It just became a thing I did when I felt stressed or overwhelmed with emotion and needed a release. Most of the time I'd find myself writing these late at night when I couldn't sleep. My brain rambling on about who knows what had happened or a thought triggered by some occurrence I hadn't yet processed. And one day, I happened to look and see just how many I had written. Now, I've never classified myself as a poet, but healing is so important to me. I hope these words help you heal too if you are hurting or give you guidance to help another. Know you are worth healing for.

Though as you read, I ask you to not feel bad or shower these pages with pity as I look for that no longer. During this process I have found that my victimhood no longer served me. These moments have now become, just.....things. Events. Happenings. To someone who was lost, lonely and afraid. Who did not know how to ask for help from the things she hadn't the words for. Who was confused about life, its purpose and her path. To a kid who was just looking for a hero, not knowing all along that the hero was within her.

As you read, I ask you to just walk with her. To be a listening ear. To acknowledge your own emotions that may arise and question their foundation. Where did that come from? Why is this making me feel this way? Ask yourself the questions others never thought of, so you can learn yourself better than before. Maybe keep a notebook nearby to write down those passing thoughts.

Now, why is healing a gradient, you ask? Because, I feel it is in direct correlation to how much pressure we feel is being applied to us or how much pressure we are putting on ourselves due to what we have been or are going through. Though, it is not always clear. Sometimes that pressure may be heavy and feel defeating. Other times it may be light and almost non-existent, those are the best days. But, just like life, a gradient has levels and stages. Using a gradient to visualize your healing and your emotions may help to give you clarity of your feelings and your progress on this journey. How much pressure you apply to a piece of paper as you shade in a gradient can be a representation of how you are feeling inside.

No matter the stage you are at on your healing journey when you find this book, remember that gradients have many shades and many levels. Only you can truly determine what each value means for you in your life. Remember that your life will continue to have ups and downs along the way. You could feel light one day and heavy the next. But, perhaps, documenting how you feel can help you become more validated in your emotions. And by keeping track of these feelings over time, you can see that good days exist, and that tough times don't last forever when doubt creeps in.

I hope that as you read these poems, you find yourself a bit more if you've been feeling lost. That you see healing of some form is always possible. To see that, you'll only lose if you stop trying. That you find some insight in the included reflections to help guide you or comfort you in your own healing.

Thank you for being here.

I’m so happy this book found you.

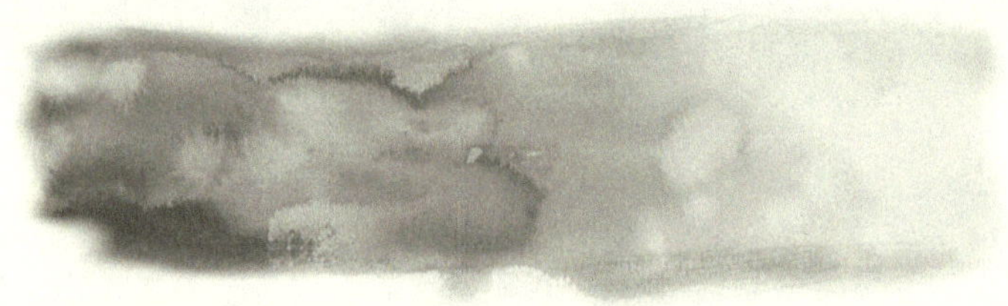

Pain

Into The Darkness

Into the darkness of my mind
Absent of feeling
Absent of time
No sense of self
No amount of wealth
In who I am
Lost once again
At times life is clear but shrouded in fear
Into the darkness
Only pain and hurt linger here
Not one smile
Not one laugh
Joy a mystery
Only memories of a traumatic history
Locked in
To
This
Darkness
Enter only if you dare

It's Scary In Here

Never feeling safe in this place
I carry it with me day to day
I try to run but I'm stuck
Cold
Alone
Wanting to go "home"
I wish I could disappear
Physically
Because mentally I'm drowning
So much pain hidden inside this brain
Layers of turmoil
Hurt
Disdain
No matter how I try it keeps going back
To that place
That dark place
It's deep
No light shines
Except the headlights I visualize
Going out
Rest sounds so good now
Can I stay there forever?
I wish
But I can't have both
I know this
But still I wish
It would just stop
Because
I'm scared
Feeling powerless to this part of me
That is me
That knows me
I think
I'm thinking

About going away
But was I ever really here?
Have I ever felt alive?
These questions render me
Helpless
A loss of breath
Gasping
struggles to breathe
Shaking
Trembling
Is this the end?
I'm scared
I want to get out
But also to be let in
Which of these is set to win?
Only time will tell
I hope I'm soon to feel well
Because
It's scary in here

You So Wrong
Girl, you so wrong
Why you always so wrong?
Wrong choice
Wrong way
Wrong person
Wrong day
Why you even feel this way?
It's wrong
You think you're right? Wrong
You think you're strong? Wrong
You think you're tough? Wrong
Girl, you so wrong
Oh girl, what's wrong?
You don't believe in self?
You don't see your wealth?
You don't trust yourself?
Wrong, wrong, wrong
Girl, you so wrong
Just do something right
Live your life
Make a choice for you
What you gone do?
Be wrong?
Girl, you so wrong
There you go again, honey
Your wrong is too much for me
You don't hear, you don't see
That's wrong
But how do I trust me?
How can I possibly see?
When all I can be, is wrong?
Even when I think I'm right, wrong
Feeling like I don't belong
No place for me

Can’t speak clearly
I don’t understand
Why can’t you see
I don’t trust me?
Because, I’m always wrong
Look at my life and where I’ve come from
So much wrong has been done
Right is wrong and wrong is wrong
Fighting each day to go on
But maybe that’s wrong
Be still
Don’t move
No choices
Too soon
Wait
And maybe one day, you won’t be wrong
But don’t wait too long, that’d be wrong
Enjoy your life, that’s right
But how, if all I feel is wrong?
Man, why am I always wrong?

Doubt can be worse than fear sometimes. Doubt keeps you from believing you can even start. Doubt says, it won't work, even if I tried. On the other hand, fear says, I'm not sure how this will go, but I'll try it anyway. Fear can still be open to success and growth while doubt is tied to failure and hopelessness. If you must choose one to lean into, choose fear.

I Hurt Myself Today

I hurt myself today
Trying to take the pain away
Exhausted and frozen
I no longer want to stay
In this place
In this body
With this mind
Lost
Forgotten
Empty
All of the same that follows it
The memories that tie it down
To a place that hurt me
Broke me
Shattered my spirit
I hurt myself
I hurt myself
I hurt myself
Too many times to count
I hurt myself today
I want to get out!
Do you hear me screaming?!
Is it you or I who's dreaming?
Wake up!
I hurt myself
Wake up!
I hurt myself
Wake up!
I hurt myself
And yet, I still feel nothing.

My Pain Is Stuck
How do I get this pain out?
It hurts
It hits me when I'm not looking
Or thinking that it would
As soon as things are looking up
When I think I'm doing good
Maybe I can scream it out
But what if others hear?
The sound of my pain could shock them
Or force them into fear
Maybe I could run it out
But I fear it'd follow me
Always catching up, never setting me free
Maybe I could cry it out
This I've tried and tried
But for only a moment of relief from my flowing teary tide
Perhaps I can sleep it away
Wake up on another day
Or forget it all within a dream
I must get this pain unstuck from me
But with all I've tried I've come to see
This pain is what keeps shaping me
Its made me love and made me live
Open my heart, learn to give
Have fun and be free
Trust and believe
That my life is beautiful and I'm worthy to be
This pain is stuck
Though I fight to shake it away
I am thankful for its lessons
For showing me the way

Releasing pain can feel like an endless journey that you may never know if you've finished. Waiting for that next trigger. Constantly running from it all. After a while we have to learn that running only makes things worse. We must learn to sit with our pain. Honor it and who we were when it happened. Give that version of you a voice to be heard, seen, to be acknowledged for what they experienced.

Insecurity

I don't feel good about me
I've got that insecurity
Doubtful who I am is enough
Am I beautiful?
Am I strong?
Am I tough?
Enough
To
Brave your gaze?
In other ways
In other words
Why are you looking at her?
Is she smarter?
Is she brighter?
Does life with her seem lighter?
Than
With me?
Insecurity
Maybe it's just my mind
Tricking me
Sticking me
Where it hurts
My heart questions what's real
Never certain how you feel
But is it really yours if someone could so easily
Steal
It away
From you?
Never certain what is true
Insecurity
I hate you

February The 14th

I didn't realize it but I was planning to leave today
Leave this world and all of you
Feeling so unloved
Lost
Blue
It happened fast
Quick
Like a switch
A choice I didn't know I had chosen
I stood there in a daze
Broken
Frozen
Fallen
Empty
Slowly going
Calling to say goodbye and hello in the same moment
But some things must fully crumble to be born again
For that moment was not my time
Still work to do
To achieve what's mine
Grateful I was saved
To live another day
Blessed to breathe
Blessed to believe
I'll keep going
To find the reason
I'm still here

A prayer for anyone struggling.

Dear Lord,
I pray that anyone who has reached the place where they feel they are no longer for this world, who sees only darkness ahead, who feels they have nothing left to give or live for, finds you. I pray they find strength to try again. Courage to believe, seek, to trust in you. May you show them that this is not it. Show them the tools, the way, their perseverance. Remind them they've already made it too far to give up now. Be the light that they are searching for so they may see tomorrow and the next. Help them to see their power, their purpose. That they are needed, valued and loved by you and many they have yet to meet. Bring them comfort and safety so they too can be a light for others in need. In Jesus' name I pray.

Amen.

Don’t Be Afraid

Don’t be afraid little child
You can rest here
Lies
Don’t be afraid little child
I’ll protect you
Disguise
Don’t be afraid little child
You can close your eyes
Fear
Don’t be afraid little child
You can trust me
Insincere
Don’t be afraid little child
Hold my hand
Deceit
Don’t be afraid little child
Have a drink
Sneak
Don’t be afraid little child
Do you mind?
Creep
Don’t be afraid little child
Don’t be afraid
Don’t be afraid
Don’t be afraid
Don’t be afraid

Trust is not something that comes easily. It takes time and patience to establish. What can deceive us is the title someone holds and thinking that grants them a certain level of trust and respect. In life we learn that not everyone deserves this. But, also, just how quickly trust that was given can go away.

Blue

When I was small blue was all
Blue was my rug, blue was my walls
But you loved it too
Blue was also you

Then you were gone, and blue went away
Gone in a second, no goodbyes to say
No longer an expression but a feeling inside
A madness of pain I tried to hide
My brokenness consumed me
I struggled for air
A feeling deep down, too painful to share

This color I loved was no longer mine
Lost in a moment, stuck in a bind
Until grace and time healed me enough to see
That this beautiful color could also be me

Until I let go of the pain you caused
When I opened my eyes
From this lingering pause
Reclaiming it all
Starting anew
I'm rebuilding myself
And I'm starting with blue

Guilt

Sometimes I feel guilty when I don't
Celebrate you like others do
But my story is not theirs
I fall apart
Conflicted
Torn
A completely shattered heart
My mind battling to find peace
To understand why I must endure this feat
What lessons must I learn for it to go away?
What task to do, what words to say?
It's been so long
I'm tired now
I want it to stop
But I don't know how

She Was Not Alone

She was not alone when God called her home
A celebration at hand, its true purpose unknown
Though we had in mind how the day would go
The Lord's plan is private
To us, He'll never show
She was not alone
We were all there
Laughter, love and joy in the air
Familiar voices and faces filled the room
Little did we know, He'd be calling soon
And though we may search for reasons why
To understand
To beg and try
To make sense of life and its uncertainty
She who once was, now a memory
But she was not alone
We were all there
To see her off
To the clouds up where
Some had been waiting for her to arrive
Though we may still be here breaking inside
She was not alone
She was loved
And she loved as deep as one could
An angel on Earth spreading mountains of good
She was not alone
When God took her hand
And guided her on to the Promised Land

- *To Arlene*

Her Tears

Her tears are like daggers
You know, the sharp kind
The ones that mar your heart
The ones that scar your mind
You see them when you're sleeping
They burn holes in the floor
Seeing her spirit broken
Happiness closing a door
Her tears sing as they fall
A sad spirit song
One that longs for those who've passed
Clinging to what has gone

A Moment

It's only a moment
But what's a moment when you feel like you're drowning?
A thousand forevers in a second
Overwhelmingly exhausting
Taxing, costly
Struggling to breathe
Fighting to live
To be present again
Doubtful you'll win
This reoccurring battle of sadness
Seems unyielding when you're feeling consumed
Praying that help will arrive soon
A moment of forever never ends quick enough
When it's full of pain

Disconnected

Here I go, in my head again
I'm in this world but I feel dead again
No sensation
No air let in
I hold on to that last breath
Before my descent into this living death
Disconnected from it all
Don't move
Feeling small
Am I breathing?
Barely
But I'm alive…right?
How can you win with no urge to fight?
I'd like to get out now.
HELLO!
Nobody's home
Alone
Even when I'm not alone
Busy tone
To my heart
My mind
You can not call
Feeling small
Wait, am I breathing?
Hardly
Who am I?
What is this?
Is this me?
Stuck in this outer body
Experience-less existence
Desensitized to life
I'm trying to wake up!
Wake up now!
Come to life!

Live!!!
Breathe!!!
I want to get up!
I'm frozen!
Thaw me!
Help!
I'm screaming!
Don't you hear me?!
Maybe a tear will help you see me
Am I breathing?
No, I'm wreathing
Twisted into knots not soon to be undone
Can't move
Can't run
But I don't want to sit with this anymore
God, please, where's the other door?
The one that leads to joy and love
Light
Ah, light me on fire so I might feel
Wait, is this real?
Where am I?
Who am I?
Fear
I'm riddled with it
To my core, I cannot break from it
Never safe or secure
Destroyed by hearts impure
Snap out of it!!!
Let's go!
Heal!
Smile!
It's FINE!
No, it's too painful to bear
I'll just sit and stare
Disconnected

Because maybe, if I can’t feel it
It can’t hurt me…

A poem about dissociation. Feeling like you're watching your life like a movie through your own eyes. What's worse is I feel I've lived most of my life this way and still battle with it at times. Being present. There were many periods in my life I didn't want to be. I didn't want to fully experience the things happening to me or around me. It is a tough habit to break when life overwhelms you even as you grow older. Just know there is light on the other side. You can learn to safely feel again.

Questions

Where Am I Going?

Where am I going?
God, please show me the way.
I feel like I'm running in circles
Getting lost in the day
Distracted and confused
Spirit broken, heart bruised
Feeling frozen, afraid to move
Where am I going?
What decision to choose?

Decisions, Decisions

Why is it so hard to decide?
This or that?
When or where?
Should I go this way or should I go there?
Is it my heart or my gut I should follow?
The thought of failure, a pill I hate to swallow
Believing in me seems so impossible
How could I be successful?
Successfully, Me
But who am I?
Sometimes I think I know, but as time goes on
The changes I show
Confuse me and make it hard to choose
No time to waste, not a day to lose
So I must decide
And make it right
For no matter which way
I will be my light

Many days I have struggled with questioning if I'm making the right decisions. Not just for myself but for my family and future me as well. It can be difficult to decipher if the choice I feel like I should make is truly for me or if it's for someone else. And that someone else could be someone in the present or past versions of myself that lurk around in my subconscious waiting for their time to shine. What I've come to realize is, I just have to turn whatever decision I make into the right one for now. Now, this could mean the decision leads me to where I wanted to go (not always likely, but sometimes I get lucky), or it shows me that new path or just turns into a lesson I can hold onto for later. Either way, I know I have to be brave enough to try, to make the choice whatever it may be and not remain frozen.

Who Are You….. Really?

A loaded question, right?
Do you mean who I am in the day or in the night?
When I'm regretting what I've done wrong
When I thought I was right?
Who I am when I'm challenged or too scared to fight?
Or maybe it's when I love too deeply and hold on too tight
Letting go is my constant struggle
Though once achieved, delight
Oh, you mean when my desire to win
Sends me spiraling when I fall
When I drag myself to the ground
Trying to show the doubters how I stand tall
Nah, you mean the one who stops listening
When someone plucks a trigger
Making that hole in my heart grow bigger and bigger
Hold on, its gotta be the one who wants to show
Love like no other
But can't for fear imbedded from a busy mother
Wait, its gotta be the one who's tried so many things
Who hates the idea they're getting used to how failure stings
Or maybe it's the one who is scared to show their shadow
Because then how can I protect myself
From all they may know?
Or it could just be this question has no way
It asks you to box yourself into who you are today
Tomorrow may lead me to a place I never dreamed
To a space where who I really am is way more
Than this in between

Discovering who you are will always be a never ending journey. One filled with ups and downs, experiences and lessons. Try not to get too hung up on where you are right now. Life is still working on you. Usually, when I get caught up in trying to define myself, I like to imagine if I were to stop any further growth or changes in my life, would I be happy, doing this, being who I am in this moment for the rest of forever? And 99.9% of the time, the answer is, 'NO'. I want to continue to see what I'm capable of. I want to keep exploring and learning new things. I'm excited to see how I will evolve as life goes on.

Where Are You, Joy?

Joy?
Why are you hiding, joy?
I was getting used to you being around.
Please come back, joy
Don't play coy, joy
Playing with my heart like a toy
I need you, hurry, joy
I'm falling again

As I started to pay closer attention to myself, my triggers and my overall mood, I became more aware of when I would start to feel an overwhelming sense of dread and just overall unhappiness. It became easier to point it out when I would have joyful times. I'd be more aware of when I felt low because I missed the awe of joy. The beauty and the excitement of joy. I started to work on my introspection and I'd ask myself, "when's the last time I was happy?". And from there I could start to look back at my timeline and see where I fell off track. Was it the snarky comment from the "supposed-to-be-friend", was it the person who cut me off in traffic or because I didn't realize I hadn't worked out or stuck to my routine. Whatever the case, asking myself that simple question in those moments allowed me to reflect, to check in with myself, forgive me for not being aware then, while also congratulating myself for recognizing I was missing something now. At times even a small trigger could have me frozen for weeks. The sooner I can catch myself falling, the easier it is for me to come back to life.

Awakening

The Wounds I Had to Heal

You'd never believe how many there were
The sleepless nights
Eyes filled with tears
The world a blur
Do not envy where I am
You have not seen where I've been
It broke me to my core
Lying empty on the floor
Shattered more than I thought real
These lingering wounds I had to heal
I'd wish them on no other
Though I leave space for how they've shaped me
In healing these wounds I opened the door
To start the journey of becoming who I'm meant to be

Trauma Talkin'

Who's that saying they hate me?
Must be my trauma talkin' again
Doubting who I can be because of where I've been

Who's that pushing everyone away thinking they're trying to
Tear me down or don't care what I say?
Must be my trauma talkin' again
Telling me my voice has no place in this world I live in
Trying to block the way

Who's that saying I should give up because
Once again I find myself stuck?
Not sure which way that I should go
Wishing my life was an easy flow
Must be my trauma talkin' again
Telling me to quit before I begin
That I'm bound to fail so why try at all?
Reminding me how it feels to fall

Over time I've learned this voice can be a gift and also a curse
It's intention to protect though many times it hurts
My light, my spirit, my hopes and dreams
Pushing me to hide myself
Afraid to be seen

But I'm tired of my trauma talkin'
Keeping me from life, I start walkin'
Away from it and the pain it's caused
When I've hurled it at others with no just cause
Afraid of what they'd do to me
If they could truly see my vulnerability

Now it's time for that trauma to stop talkin'
To start walkin' and let me be

For when I release this trauma
I’ll truly be free

Here Is Not It

This ain't it
Not them
Not you now
Not you here
There's more work to do
Before you find the place that's set for you
When they don't hear you or see you
Know this is true
You'll be heard and seen by those
Who choose to make a place for you
Don't allow yourself to be used by those undeserving
Save your truth and your gifts for those that are worthy
Your voice is powerful, magical and true
Love yourself right where you are
As you're becoming you

Stop Running

Girl, where you going again?
Ain't you tired of all that running?
No place to hide
They follow you
All of your problems stuck like glue
To your soul and your heart
Your mind when it's dark
Heavy on your chest
Stuck in your throat
A part
From it all you wish you were free
But freedom only comes when you stop running
And open your eyes so you can see
The hurts and pains lingering
From your past that keep draining you still
It's time to stop running
Say that you will

3am

That's when you call
Ears ringing
Left and right
High and low
Telling me which way to go
Restless I wake
And listen clear
Closing my eyes to feel you near
At 3am my angels speak
Messages flowing like a creek
Slow and tumbling
Quick and flowing
Making clear what the world is showing
It's quiet now
I feel them near
Warm and safe
I hold them dear

It's Crazy How Crazy

My life is
Smiling day to day
Bringing joy to others
While inside my soul is smothered
With pain
Doubt, hurt, confusion, mistrust
Used and abused
Cast aside
Fading to dust
How can you possibly smile?
He did what to you?
They did what to who?
Inside I burn from the fire of my anger
Don't poke this bear
I will go crazy
Because It's so crazy
How crazy
My life is
Telling my story would scare most beyond
Telling tales they could never dream upon
I wish they were dreams
I would have woken up sooner
Thankful for the awakening of healing
My crazy life presents
Me, crazy
I should be, obviously
But why be oh so crazy
When my life could have so much beauty
A deeper love than ever before
A hand to hold
Children to adore
Oh no
THIS is crazy
Not in a million years would I believe

A greater purpose was set for me
Joy unmeasured
Growth together
Dreams, aspirations
Experiences surmount
Mountains of love awaiting me
It’s crazy how crazy
My life is

I Can't Remember

Most of it's a haze
Dark, mysterious
A maze
Can't remember if I went left or right
Safety and clarity
Out of sight
Maybe it's just my body protecting me
My brain refusing to let me see
How dark it truly was
It's crazy what the body does
To save itself
From the reality of what it's been through
But, hey, do you remember
When you went to that place?
Won that race?
Saw their face?
Sometimes I feel so lost in space
An emptiness that suffocates my memories
But part of me wonders
Is it best that I should see?
Because isn't my body just protecting me?
So I don't hurt
No pain would it willingly exert on itself
Covered in dust on the shelf
Of my soul
Still deep inside
Waiting for light to guide me on my way
So maybe, it can be healed
But first, I must remember

When I Can’t Sleep

Can’t sleep
Mind tangled in clouded knots
Confused
Unsure
Make it stop
I’m so tired
Just begging to drift off into nothingness
Mind be empty
Be clear
But all I can think of, see, hear
Is all the things I did not say
Anxiety pulling me away
Closed off from my lips
Stuck in my mind
I can’t sleep
Shaking ensues
Panic
Hold on
Losing it
Bottled up about to burst
Tears flood my face
How do I say it
I can’t
But it hurts me down inside
Hide
All your feelings
They’re not valid anyway
No one really cares
Will they hear me
Probably not
Closed off and shrinking
Not a peep
What’s wrong?
I stall

Nothing, just tired

But, I still can't sleep

Back And Forth

Back and forth I go
Remaining here or trying to grow
Old habits
Triggers
Holding me down
Stay still they say
Stay this way
I yearn to break free from their grasp upon me
Stuck in a mind frozen in time
Years pass by
Time is fleeting
When will I wake up
To negative thoughts retreating
Soon I hope
Because, with all of this back and forth
I can't cope

528

Frequency speak to me
Heal me from within
Remove me from the pain
Of all the places I have been
Heal my mind
Reveal a time
When I am born anew
Breathe new life
And give me sight
Of all that I must do

Fog
Mysterious
Misty
Your water droplets hit me
As I walk through you
The world gets clearer
The further I proceed
But too far ahead
I can not see

I keep walking

Along this journey of healing I have found myself feeling like I'm stuck in a fog. A haze of not knowing where I'm going and, at moments, too far ahead to see all the places I've been. It can be scary. To learn to trust has been the most difficult thing when I have had to re-learn what it means. When safety and reassurance were not ingrained in my childhood. It can be messy. It can be daunting to think of moving forward despite it all. Have you ever stood in fog? It leaves a bit of mist on you. Sometimes unnoticeable. I think life works that way. We don't always know what the moments we experience will leave behind until we take a look. Some may stay longer than others, some may melt away. But, all of it makes up the journey. The fog.

And sometimes that fog is ever present in our mind when the world becomes too much. When it's too painful to look back or look forward. I have learned to find beauty in that. Being focused on the present. What is right in front of me. That next first step in whatever direction feels right. I have learned to embrace those foggy times. They have taught me to trust in the Universe and its guidance. Sometimes it shows up when I'm spending too much time thinking about the past or my future. When I need to show up for me right now. I can't change what's happened. And what's to come will only be if I take the next first step and keep moving. Not in fear. But, with the belief that beautiful things are waiting for me.

Releasing

I let it go today
I closed my eyes
And said what I needed to say
The ringing
The buzzing
Left
Right
Left
Right
I fell deeper into the space between reality and
The visions that follow me
Of things past that scarred me so viciously
Cyclically
Over and over reminding me of pain endured
I closed my eyes
Tears flowing
I said, “no more”
I let you go today
I said goodbye to the way you hurt me
Left me in the dark
Too afraid to speak and clear my heart
But I made peace with you today
And let you gently float away
In every tear that fell down my face
I released you to make space
For new joy and light and memories
To make space for what I wish my life to be

EMDR

EMDR saved my life. It was the first type of therapy I felt dug right into what was keeping me stuck. It taught me how to effectively tune out the noise so I could see the problem and not to just shut down to the world. To myself. To remain present with the pain so I could heal it. Release it. It also showed me that I am capable of healing. EMDR changed me. It helped me make space in my mind and my soul for the guidance that God and the Universe had been wanting to share with me for so long. Or more so, brought me closer to what I had forgotten from my childhood. It broke those repeating cycles. Tore up the calendar of my pain that would remind me year after year how I hurt on this day. Not all memories need to be constantly honored. For some, once is enough. EMDR showed me that letting go of pain is possible. Now, I'll never forget those things that happened, but they don't hurt as bad when I'm reminded of them. And for that, I'll forever be grateful.

Trauma Ties

Trauma ties us down
And holds us back
Not letting go
Giving no slack
It reminds you of your past pain
The dark and lonely days
No sunshine
Just rain
It drives you down a never ending road
Of torment and sadness
Nowhere to go
It lives inside you waiting to be seen
Only to be heard when you start to scream
It cries to be noticed
To be real
To be accepted
For that is the only true way
To get where you are headed
The trauma you faced is tied to your soul
Shifting and shaping you as you grow old
Until you decide to finally say
Trauma
Your hold on me ends today

Healing

Healing Is A Gradient

When I first thought this
I wasn't sure what it meant
I know what a gradient is and how it is formed
But how is it like healing
Or being reborn?
Perhaps it's the slow change from dark to light
The gentle releasing
As you begin to take flight
A steady growth as life gets a bit lighter
Moving out from the darkeness
Things get a bit brighter
But if you go back to the stages before
And shade them again with life once more
The darkness creeps in
And you must start again
Down a treacherous road
From whence you've been
But, healing is a gradient
Go slow and steady
Keep a light hand
Move on when you're ready
Don't move too fast
Or you'll miss what's necessary
To truly let go of what keeps you weary
The things that tie you down
And shield your eyes from life
That keep you bogged down in a history of strife
And though it may seem so far away
Seeing healing as a gradient
Is a reminder
The light will come one day

I Wore Blue

Today I wore blue
And didn't think about you
At least
I don't think
Today I wore blue
Because once it was for you
But no more
Today I wore blue
To heal
Remembering how it once made me feel
To wear blue
To not be blue
But to be me in blue
Today I wore blue
And I feel thankful
I do
That I can again, wear blue
And not think of you

I’m Not Okay

You’re okay, you’ll be okay
It doesn’t have to hurt all day
Just take a breath
And find a way to feel the words you cannot say
To ground yourself so you don’t fall
As you fight again to break this wall
Of pain so deep you cannot breathe
A world so dark you cannot see
As you pray it eases and starts to go
When will it stop, you do not know
But you’ll be okay, just give it time
Breathe in deeply and clear your mind
Give yourself space and time to be
You’ll be okay
This
I guarantee

Hey

I thought I could just say, “Hey”, to you
But here I am a mess
I thought I could make it quick
But no, that pain still hit
Like bricks
I’m broken once more
Head down
Tears on the floor
Why?
Why then, why now, why you?
Who am I?
I feel lost every time my mind lingers here
In that darkness
Reaching for the parts of me that went with you
Will I ever heal?
When can I feel
Again?
These times are always troubling, anxiety growing
Will it last forever this time?
Can I get back to me in an hour?
Will this fight take me too?
I pray it doesn’t
I pray I’m strong
I pray for the day
I can say, “Hey”, and it won’t take my light away

Backslide

I fell back
And not in a good way
I fell back into that pain
Chaos
It hurt
It still hurts when it hits
Not just for me but those around me too
I'm sorry
I fell back again
I thought it was gone but it still lingers
On
On my heart, my mind, my soul
Why won't it release its control on
Me
Set me free
Leave me be
You are so far behind, but just won't let
Go
I release it all
You're free too
I carry you no longer
Holding on to you does not make me stronger
I want to live my life as the me I choose to be
To create beauty
Love and light
To know when and why not to fight
I refuse to carry on this dance with you
You do not win
Here is where you end
This backslide will not be my demise
I will rise
I will fight
For those I love

For what I deserve
Continue to serve and give light
Not in hindsight
But before
Sight
Unseen, divine, green
Growth continued
To find a new way to be
Continually

Healing is messy. Have you ever paid attention to how a wound heals? How long it can take depending on how deep it is? It's all the same, whether physical, emotional, or otherwise. It takes time. And even when the scab falls off once it's hardened over, the healing is still incomplete. Be patient with yourself during this time.

Stages of Grief

I know there are five of these but I think I’m in a mix of two
I’m feeling depressed and immensely angry over you
Being
Gone
I feel like I’m in a haze
Quiet moments feel like ages
Lost
Searching for your light only to find
An emptiness where you once were
I miss you
I’ve denied it all
Pleaded for your return
Accept it to be true?
I don’t know if I can
Not yet
My heart will not let me let you go
But I will speak to you
And reach for you
Think of you when my heart is low
For your presence was always a safe place to go

Triggered

Here it goes again
I thought I was strong again
Guess I was wrong again
Two weeks or more of this again
Crying curled in a ball again
It's like I'm on that road again
That night when I went numb again
I want to see the sun again
But I just feel so stuck again
So dumb again
Thought that I could run again
From this pain so deep I'm broken again
I need this agony to stop again
So I can start to breathe again
Feel again
Live again

On the healing journey there will come a time when life will test you, to see if you've truly healed, if you've truly grown from that thing you said you wanted to let go of. And what we will find, sometimes, is that we may not be as healed as we thought. And.....that is okay. What I've found works best is measuring. Did I stay in this cycle as long as last time? If the answer is, "No", I know I'm growing. It's a long process. Do not rush it. Give yourself grace and be thankful that you're still here to try again. To keep working on you. The world needs you.

Growth

Access Denied

Access denied
Doesn't mean you never tried
But the hurt you caused
Made a great divide
In my trust for you
It's more than money
More than words
Same ole' actions
Continue to occur
No accountability
You truly just don't see
It is a privilege to have access to me

Where I'm Supposed to Be

When I imagine my future
I see it clear as day
And where I am today is not where I want to stay
The troubles that I face seem distant
And menial
Many times I fail to see what this challenge is really for
I forget that life is a path you must take
Every step of it counts
No passes
No breaks
No jumps ahead
No cuts or advances
Each day a new task, an opportunity for chances
When clarity comes forth on those cloudy days
It helps me see when I have made an error in my ways
When I must turn around to face a danger behind me
Before I can move on to where I'm supposed to be

This poem is one that brings up many emotions when I think about my healing journey. I know many people have said not to look back and keep moving forward. But, I think at times we must turn around to see what it is that keeps holding us back. That string on our shirt that got caught years ago, slowly unraveling as we go along, eventually to leave us bare. We must cut the cord. And to do so, face that pain and say, "no more". I have had to look back many times to find clarity, assess triggers and most of all to reconnect with my inner child who I lost along the way. Sometimes looking back can be the best way to confidently move forward. Once I was able to locate my inner child and remind myself of the dreams I had back then and what brought me joy, I could honestly begin to help her heal.

Finding Him

I went searching for Him again
After I lost her
Confused and needing clarity
I reached for His hand to guide me
Needing to feel stability
Reassurance
To feel whole

I knew Him once before
Before life blocked my view
For many countless years
I had forgotten what God can do
I walk with Him now
Let him guide my steps
Show me which path to take
Tell me when I need rest

I found Him again, when I lost her
Seeing the light that is my life
Finally seeing my worth
I proudly step forward
Into this season of my life's rebirth

The Seed

Was it all for not
A waste of time
Why did I open up this
Crazy, stupid, naive, insecure, dumb, ridiculous
Heart of mine?
Another dangling carrot
Never to grasp
What I thought was it
Now gone so fast
But here I go again
Miss all or nothing
Constantly worried I won't amount to something
Trying ever so persistently to succeed
To be loved
To be seen
To be all "they" need
When at the end its me
Yep, just me that I need
To love and support, to believe in
The seed
That was planted in my soul
Before I became "Me"
Not to deter or second guess
A path laid Universally
A destiny, if you will
Carved out in time
When will I see
That it's already mine?
You've got all you need
No place for greed, doubt, or jealousy
I must trust in the Universe's plan for me
Believe in the seed that was planted in your soul
Before you were you, before you grow old
Do you hear the message?

I hope that you do
Now, when will you start believing in you?

Forgive Yourself

Forgive yourself for the choices you made
For on that path you could not stay
You had to break through and start again
Though neither of us knows how or when
Life will force us to begin anew
Present us a new array of things to do
But we must first make amends
So we can start to live again
Forgive yourself for who you were
Without peace
And life a blur
Forgive yourself for what you did not know
See how it was needed for you to grow
For life has a balance we must learn
To see the strength in the scars we earn
That the sight of them means you survived
Forgive yourself
And begin to thrive

There's Always

A new friend to make
Chances to take
Goals to set
Habits to break
People to admire
Friends to inspire
When you are working on you
Only keep in your life
What makes your soul feel true

Dream

Sometimes I can't help but dream
Imagining things never once seen
How can I make this come to be?
But also, God,
You see this in me?
Dreams can be seen as visions from the divine
Springing up in a moment
Lost in time
Guiding you ahead on your path of life
Only you can decipher what is right
What choice to make
Which path to take
Which version of you that must break
To bring forth the vision planted in your soul
Dreams are visions of mini goals
To keep you striving for something more
A new lesson to learn
A new opened door
To build you up to who you're meant to be
Don't wait too long
It's time to dream

I Believe I Am

I believe I am
Worthy of a great life
Destined to be a great light
Built strong yet soft
Tough and bright
Brave enough to win this fight
Between my mind and heart
No longer standing
Afraid to start
Living the dreams I see so clearly
To release the hesitation
Belief without procrastination
So I can step into the version of me
That I'm truly destined to be
I believe I am
Worthy
Deserving
Releasing all doubt
From the top of my lungs I shout
I believe I am!

They Danced

Across the sky they danced
While I stood in a trance
Back and forth
Left and right
Their wings outstretched
Engulfed in flight
Their calls of joy
Soaring to and fro
I delight in their life
A beautiful show

Two herons dance across the sky as I stand in the garden. I felt present in this movement. I looked up. I saw life. I admired it. I held space for it.

It was beautiful.

Glow

You are shining
You glow
Radiant and poised
Standing tall you guide
Others find you in their darkness
Bright and warm
A home
A fire burning brightly
You are already who you are to become
It’s only hidden inside of you
I see your light and hold space

Everyone has a gift and a purpose in this life if you're willing to see what it is they're here to teach us. Even you.

What can you teach the world?

I Am
Loving
Caring
Helpful
Needed
Thoughtful
Intelligent
Dependable
Reliable
Kind
Worthy
Talented
Beautiful
Loved
Calm
Aware
Me

Believe

Do you believe in you?
You should
Why do you think others are the only ones
With good
Who get good
Who can do good?
You should
Believe in you
Who told you
You can't
You won't
Don't?
It's not possible?
Only because their brain can't see
What you can do if you just believe
Take the leap

Be Bold

Be bold this year
Be brave, no fear
No hesitation
No procrastination
Your opportunity is
Right
Here
The time is now
Go forth, head high
For you must first jump
To reach the sky

My Garden Taught Me Life

My garden taught me life
And not in the way you'd think
It taught me about the things
That made me drown and sink
That brought me down and held me back
From who I need to be
That too much of a "good" thing was slowly breaking me
That hiding imperfections kept me away from so much good
That the spots on me are golden
Proof I've lived life as I should
That through it all I'm here
I've kept going and stayed strong
My garden taught me life
What I wish I'd known all along
That sunshine is key
Drink water freely
Remove what's draining you
And have friends that support you too
To trust in the process and believe that each plant knows
Its purpose in this life is only but to grow
And in that growth it provides for those
Who appreciate its worth
To believe in the connection each plant has to this Earth
That our human interference can cause more harm than good
To relax and let be
Trust nature to stand as it has always stood
My garden taught me life
In more ways than one
My garden taught me life
Now I bathe under the sun

Be patient in all you do
Because, from beginning to end, you need time to grow too

I'm Still Here

Sometimes I'm not sure why
But, I'm still here
Navigating it all
The joy
The fear
Seeing the light
When the dark rolls in
Accepting that life allowed me to start again
Finding peace in all that's transpired
Looking to Him when I get tired
Believing in more than what my pain has left
The many scars of sadness, regret
Knowing that through life
We may die and live many times over
Versions of ourselves changing as we grow older
I look for the lessons and clear the path ahead
By learning to live with the memories I dread
That sneak up on me as time passes on
Studying so deeply where I went wrong
Trying to heal a broken me
A person far gone, lost at sea
Reading the tears that fall from my face
Into my hands I hold them with grace
Leaning surely into the stories they tell
Though together they could fill a well
But, I'm still here
And with that I must know
That someone above said I still need to grow
That I'm strong enough to see this through
That I am here
And there's work to do

2/13/25

I wrote this poem the day before the 13th anniversary of my suicide attempt. At a time when I was feeling like I really needed to accept that there has to be a bigger plan for my life, otherwise, I should not have lived from that experience. When 2/14 rolls around, I get so many mixed feelings. Of course, for one, it's Valentine's Day. The day everyone is supposed to feel loved the most (right?). Yet, I get conflicted with the reminder that there was a time I felt so unloved on that day, I no longer wanted to live. Not feeling loved by others was one thing, but not loving myself on top of that was the most catastrophic. And I want to clarify that I FELT unloved, because feeling unloved and being unloved are two different things.

I'm starting to think that when a person says they feel unloved, it could really be they struggle to love themselves which makes it difficult to receive any love given to them, no matter how pure. I think when people truly love themselves they set boundaries to protect them (as best as they can). And I've hardly talked about this, and definitely not publicly. Possibly due to feeling shame or a fear of crying in front of others. I now feel it is time for me to release this pain. Not to give it to anyone else, but hopefully, to show anyone battling with this that it's possible to embrace your life and find joy again. To feel love again (if not for the first time). That because you are still here, you have a purpose. And God wants you to find it. The world needs you to find it. YOU need you to find it. And you can.

I believe in you.

Go for it!

Final Thoughts

Life can deal us some crazy cards at times. Many of which we don't even realize we're holding until our world starts to crumble around us. Everything breaking, seemingly without reason. It is a troubling, confusing place to be. Over the years I have found it is in those moments when stillness is what is needed most to find the clarity to move forward. To look inward. To review our steps that have gotten us here in the first place. We have to look back. And that is the scary part.

Looking back is what initiates accountability. It pokes at faults, shines a light on habits, traditions, our innate ways of being. And when that happens we tend to think of just how much we've gotten wrong. It's hard to navigate those gray areas. Those spaces where we analyze what we've learned through all of our experiences and have to decide which ones were right, wrong, and did I make those decisions for me or someone else. In life, all things can be a mix of those and more. Sometimes it can take years to sort through the mess of it all. Looking for some sort of guidance can be exhausting, defeating and frustrating. Searching for answers that maybe those around you could never give. And whether that is because they haven't yet looked back to see how they got where they are, all you can do is stay your course.

Healing is such a personal thing, though living is not. We need community, friendships, relationships, and connections to thrive. To survive. We cannot make it alone, but time alone on the journey is important to get clearer about who we truly are. About who we truly want to be or wanted to be before the trials of life altered our trajectory. To find, in that quiet, the feelings, goals, dreams and curiosities, that fueled us as children. We must go back there. That is the place that reminds us why we choose to keep going. And in healing, we work to protect that place. It must be sacred.

It is also in that place where we can meet that higher power. And that can be whatever you wish it to be. Whether it be God, the Universe or something else entirely. Ultimately, your inner guidance. That little voice that you listen to even when you don't think you're listening. The one that makes you face those challenges you want to ignore. I think sometimes we can get more off course when we choose not to listen for fear of disappointing others, going against what we feel to be true. But, isn't that what change is about? What growth is about? To lean into the new, the different, the obscure? Become friends with not knowing what life has in store next and take the chance anyway. And trust yourself to make the next best decision when those results arise.

Over time, and through much practice, I believe we all can get better at this. Though we must also acknowledge that this will be a never ending quest. We just get better equipped to handle the next thing as we move along. While looking back can be the first step to saying you're ready to move forward, walking into the unknown, into the fog, is the real testament to your desire to be more than what you are right now. You are an ever changing work of art. Know that when you walk into a room, you carry with you all of the layers that have built you into who you are in that moment. All of the fears, joys, experiences, lessons, laughs, tears. It is with you all of the time. And you have the power to decide who you want to become in that next second, next minute, month or year, by making the next best decision for you. All you have to do is choose to begin. To choose you.

www.ingramcontent.com/pod-product-compliance
Lightning Source LLC
LaVergne TN
LVHW090534110826
845146LV00003B/1088